# PETS

## Cats, Dogs, Horses, & Camels, too!

Carus Publishing Company
Peterborough, NH
www.cricketmag.com

**Staff**
Editorial Director: Lou Waryncia
Project Editor: Charles Baker III
Designer: Brenda Ellis, Graphic Sense
Proofreader: Eileen Terrill


**Text Credits**
The content of this volume is derived from articles that first appeared in *CLICK®, APPLESEEDS,*
and *ASK®* magazines. Contributors: Susan Yoder Ackerman ("Horse Country"), Nicholas C.
Chybinski ("My Friend Rasputin"), Carolyn Gard ("What Casper Taught Me"), Meg Moss
("To Fly Without Wings"), Suzanne M. Rhinehart ("Camel"), Lynn Parrish Sutton ("Carry, Pull,
and Plow").


**Picture Credits**
Wenhai Ma: 4–5; Jeremy R. Pierce: 6; Jaime Zollars: 8; Photos.com: 9, 11, 16, 19; Dynamic
Graphics: 10; JoLynn Alcorn: 12–15, 18, 20–21; Comstock: 17; Sandy Rabinowitz 22–28


**Cover**
Dynamic Graphics

**The Library of Congress Cataloging-in-Publication Data** for *Pets* is available at
http://catalog.loc.gov.


Carus Publishing
30 Grove Street, Peterborough, NH 03458
www.cricketmag.com


Printed in China

# Table of Contents

What Casper Taught Me . . . . . 4

My Friend Rasputin . . . . . . . . . . . . . . 6

Goldie . . . . . . . . . . . . . . . . . . . . . . . . . 8

Carry, Pull, and Plow . . . . . . . . . . . . . . 9

Camel . . . . . . . . . . . . . . . . . . . . . . . . 10

Born to Run . . . . . . . . . . . . . . . . . . . .11

To Fly Without Wings . . . . . . . . . . . . .12

Becoming the Horse . . . . . . . . . . . . . .20

Horse Country . . . . . . . . . . . . . . . . . . 22

Glossary . . . . . . . . . . . 29

Map . . . . . . .30

# What Casper Taught Me

**Y**ou've got a puppy, and you're all set to teach it to come, sit, stay, and not chew up your shoes. That's great — but don't stop there. Have you ever thought that you can learn something from your dog?

Don knows this very well. On his eighth birthday, Don's grandfather gave him a puppy. Don named the puppy Casper, and Casper stayed by Don's side almost every hour of the day for nine years.

"My uncle helped me train Casper to hunt rabbits and birds," Don says. "But the dog and I didn't always hunt. After I got home from school and did my chores, Casper and I went into the woods to hike. Casper knew when we weren't hunting, and he taught me how to find animals."

Casper amazed Don because the dog cared about young animals. He never hurt the babies. If Casper found a nest of baby rabbits, he would nudge the bunnies, but he never bit them. Don started watching Casper closely.

When Casper sniffed with his nose to the ground, Don knew the dog had found the trail of a rabbit. When Casper lifted his nose and sniffed the air, Don knew he smelled a deer or a bird.

"I spent many hours with Casper," Don remembers. "Once I got mad at him, yelled, and hit him with a stick. Casper barked at me. He was telling me that we were friends and I didn't need to hit him. I never hit him again."

By spending time with Casper and rewarding him for good behavior, Don built a close bond with his dog. When Don fell out of a tree and hurt himself, Casper lay beside him and kept him company until Don could get up and walk.

"The most important thing Casper taught me was a respect for wildlife," Don remembers. "There is a time for hunting and a time for not hunting. Casper knew the difference, and the wild animals sensed when we weren't hunting. I saw much more because Casper and I were relaxed. We didn't scare the animals."

Don suggests that all dog owners take time to be with their dogs. "Train your dog to obey you, and be sure to do something fun together every day. You and your dog will be best friends for years."

# My Friend Rasputin

It was March 1941 in Europe, and I was 15 years old. I sat on my front steps enjoying a book when I saw the biggest, meanest-looking cat stroll by. It walked like the king of the jungle. There had been saber-toothed tigers among his ancestors, and their blood was still running in his veins. He was not just sneaking around corners. His muscular body was moving through the very center of the yard, his feet barely touching the ground. If there ever was a cat that ruled with a strong paw all that he patrolled, this was that cat. I named him Rasputin.

I was fascinated and spoke to him in my most polite cat language: "Hi there, handsome."

Rasputin stopped, looked me over, and raised his right eyebrow, seeming to say, "Are you talking to me?" I moved over on my step, thus inviting him to join me. He thought for a moment and came over and sat down. Then I read to him from my book, and he seemed to enjoy it. I was impressed. Here was a cat with great personality and intelligence.

The nearby mill was overrun with zillions of the biggest rats I had ever seen. Now here was a cat well able to deal with them. I got up and politely led the way to the mill. I followed Rasputin inside, hoping that he would be the answer to our rat problem.

Rasputin took great interest in the rats. I hid behind a door and watched him through a crack between the hinges. When he noticed that I was gone, he forgot the rats and went looking for me.

It took a while before Rasputin spotted my feet behind the door. He looked up into my eyes and suddenly realized that this was a wonderful game. He wanted to play it again, except that now he would hide, and I would look for him. From a standing position, he leaped high in the air with all four legs stretched out in four directions. With a shriek, he hit the ground running and disappeared. I went looking for him. When I found him, he made another leap, and shrieked, and let me run and hide. We did this for a while, taking turns hiding, and we enjoyed it greatly.

One thing I did not understand was why Rasputin never bothered the many rats in the mill. I thought that probably in the cat world, it was not polite to chase your friend's rats. If you want rats, you go find them somewhere else.

I had to leave town that summer and did not have a chance to say goodbye. I knew Rasputin would miss our games and so would I. He was a good friend, and I will never forget him.

*This is a true story written by a man from Poland who later moved to the United States, where he has continued to make many friends in the animal as well as the human world.*

That cat could be a problem.

You're right, we're goners!

Not everyone can have a horse or a dog or a cat for a pet. Some children are happy with a goldfish and have to do different things to take care of it.

# Goldie

Goldie swims around
In her goldfish bowl.
The bottom is flat.
The top is a hole.

I feed her fish crumbles
That float and then sink.
And, of course, she has plenty
Of water to drink.

She's graceful and pretty,
So orange and bright,
And if she weren't swimming,
I'd kiss her good night.

# Carry, Pull, and Plow

There's no question that machines, like cars and trucks and tractors, are handy things to have around. But, sometimes, it takes an animal to get the job done right. All over the world, people still rely on animals to help them with their work. These people often become close to their animals, and the animals become like pets.

# Camel

Galumpity bumpity roll and rock —
That's the rhythmic camel walk.
Lumpity humpity riding seat —
Traveling through the desert heat.
Whumpity thumpity quiet sound —
Padded feet touch softly down.
Itchity twitchity hairy hide —
Sure it smells, but what a ride!

**Did you know?**
Camels and their owners
are often close and know
each other like you know
your dog, cat, or horse.

# Born to Run

If a cheetah and a horse ran a race, who would win? The cheetah — it's the fastest land animal in the world and can run as fast as 70 miles per hour. Even the fastest racehorses reach speeds of only about 45 miles per hour.

But if a cheetah and a horse ran a mile race, who would win? The horse — the cheetah would have to stop less than halfway through to rest and catch its breath. The horse, however, could keep running for miles without tiring. It's built not only for speed, but also for endurance.

Like a person, a horse sweats when it runs, cooling off large areas of skin quickly. Cats and other animals with thick fur cool off by panting. If a horse cooled itself off that way, its body temperature would rise so high when it ran, that it would have to stop running or it might die.

# To Fly Without Wings

If you are a bike rider, you may remember the first time you were able to get up and go. You could now travel so much faster and farther than you ever could on foot. Off you went to your friend's house, to school, or to the park. What freedom!

The first people to ride horses probably felt the same way. According to one ancient legend, God created the horse to fly without wings. And once people began to ride horses, our lives were changed forever.

## Disappearing Herds

When did an early person first throw a leg over the bare back of a horse? Scientists aren't sure. They do know, however, that horses once ran wild through the open grasslands of Europe, Asia, and the Americas. Prehistoric people's first dealings with horses were as a source of food. Long before people learned to plant crops or raise animals,

**Did you know?**
A horse runs on tiptoe.

they were hunters who lived in caves. For food, they searched for fruits and nuts and stalked animals, including wild horses.

Then, about 10,000 years ago, soon after the end of the last Ice Age, horses disappeared completely from the Americas and from most of Europe and Asia. The exact reasons for their extinction are uncertain, but it was probably the result of weather changes and overhunting.

The only places where horses survived were the grassy plains, or steppes, stretching from eastern Europe across Central Asia to Mongolia. There, for the first time, they began to develop a bond with people that would help both horses and humans survive. Wild horses were herded, bred, and cared for by people, who would later take them to all the corners of the world.

## To Eat or to Ride?

Of all the millions of animals on earth, horses are among the handful that have been tamed by people. Dogs were tamed to keep people company and help them hunt. Sheep, goats, and cattle were used for meat and milk, and their hides and hair for clothes. Were horses first herded for similar reasons?

Some archaeologists studying sites in Central Asia where people lived 6,000 years ago think horses were indeed used as a food source. In the harsh, snowy winters of the steppes, sheep and cattle would starve unless people found food for them. But horses can feed themselves in winter, since they can dig through snow to find grass to eat, and can survive on poorer-quality food than other animals. Horses may have been used, then, to provide a steady supply of food that helped people live through the winter. To prove that ancient people herded horses for food, archaeologists are studying broken pieces of pots they've found, looking for traces of mare's milk. If people milked horses, it's likely the horses were tame. After all, who would try to milk a wild animal?

Other archaeologists think horses were tamed not to be eaten, but to be ridden. These scientists believe that ancient people hunted and ate wild horses but began to keep herds of horses only when they discovered how fast and far they could travel on horseback.

## The First Ride

No one knows when the first horseback ride occurred. Perhaps an ancient horseherder, or even a fearless youngster, hopped on the back of a friendly horse. It must have been a wild ride as the surprised horse ran off carrying the heavy weight of a human. Up top, without saddle or reins, the rider probably held on for dear life.

But riding a horse would not be very useful without a way to control it. So, archaeologists are looking for evidence of early controlled horseback riding — and they may have found it. A few small pieces of antler with holes in them have been unearthed at sites in Europe and Asia dating back

almost 6,000 years. The antler pieces are similar to cheek pieces used to hold a bit in a horse's mouth. (The bit is connected to the reins and helps a rider control the horse.) Ancient horse teeth found nearby show signs of wear that could have been made only by a bit. This leads the scientists to believe that people were not only riding their horses, but using bits and reins to do so.

## Horse Friendship

But how did people tame horses? The horses themselves probably helped. Horses are social animals. They thrive on the companionship a herd offers, and they depend on its security.

I wish I could ride a horse to school every day!

Horses in the herd establish a "pecking order," and they know who is boss. Horses communicate with one another using body language. They show friendship by grooming or scratching one another with their teeth. To show who's in charge, a horse will reach out and lower its head as if to bite, or raise a leg as if to kick. It will flatten its ears — protecting a vulnerable part of its body — to signal it's ready to fight. People were able to use similar friendly and threatening actions to establish themselves as leaders of the herd.

Horses became less popular for dinner as we began to harness their strength, energy, and speed. People put horses to work carrying packs and pulling chariots, wagons, and plows. Mounted explorers roamed for miles in search of better lands and hunting

**Did you know?**
A horse can sleep standing up because its legs can lock into place.

grounds. Covering vast distances on horseback, people of different cultures exchanged information, language, and goods. Horses made warfare easier, too. Imagine hundreds of fierce mounted raiders swooping down on your village, horses snorting and hooves clattering! Before long, people began to protect their villages and create permanent, safer

communities. And, since flowing robes or even bare legs could be uncomfortable for riding, ancient horseback riders sported a new type of clothing: pants. It would be hard to picture our world today without them!

Until the railroad train was invented many centuries later, horses remained the fastest way to travel on land. So important were these speedy steeds that the first trains were called "iron horses." It was only in the 20th century that horse power was gradually replaced by machinery and engines. Now, horses are still important to people, but as friends or for sports, not for transport or war.

Hyracotherium "Dawn Horse"  Mesohippus "Middle Horse"

# Becoming the Horse

T he horse as we know it today evolved over millions of years as it adapted to changes in the environment. Ancient horses differed in many ways, but it was how their toes, teeth, and tummies adapted that helped them survive through the centuries.

You might not recognize the fox-sized creature, which was the horse's earliest ancestor. Sometimes called "dawn horse," it developed nearly 60 million years ago. Its feet were like paws, with four toes on each front foot and three on the back. The toes were awkward for fast running, but good for traveling over the marshy land where this animal lived. Dawn horse was a browser — it nibbled the berries and soft leaves it found in the

20

*Merychippus "Premodern Horse"*     *Equus "Modern Horse"*

forest. Its teeth were too soft to chew tough grasses and plants, and its stomach couldn't digest such food anyway.

The "middle horse" developed about 35 million years ago. It was still a browser, but it was larger — the size of a sheep. It had just three toes on each foot — the middle toe being larger than the other two. Over the next 18 million years, earth's climate slowly changed. The lush forests became dry, grassy plains. And the horse changed, too. This "premodern horse" had strong teeth to grind and chew wild grasses. And its legs were long, each ending in a strong, single toe, which made it faster on the plain and able to outrun predators. Our modern horse finally developed about 3 million years ago. It was tall and fast. Its single hoof enabled it to spring forward for speed. And it had the teeth and tummy to survive on a food that was everywhere — grass.

# Horse Country

Outside the car window, the hills are covered with green grass and lined with white board fences. We're in horse country, but I'm not so sure I'm cut out for horses, even if Aunt Maggie's crazy about them. I feel in my pocket for the big red apple I'm bringing along, just in case I need it at the riding stables.

"Aunt Maggie?" I say. "I'm a little bit scared."

"Scared of horses?" She laughs. "Maybe that's a good thing, Kyle. Then you won't do something foolish like walk behind them where they might kick you, or make a loud, sudden noise. You don't want them to spook."

"Like Halloween?"

"Spook means to startle or jump up," says Aunt Maggie.

"Why do horses have to be so jumpy?" I ask. "I think I'd rather ride bumper cars. With tires that stay on the ground."

"Well, that makes sense. You're used to cars. I'm used to horses," Aunt Maggie says. "Horses are prey animals. To survive in the wild, they need to be quick. A wolf might attack, or a mountain lion. A horse has to be able to startle and rear and run away with the herd on pounding hooves."

"Just like in the movies," I say.

"Horses in a herd keep a lookout
for each other, and that's how they stay
safe. They're always on the alert. A good horse
person respects that, even in the stable. You give
them space. You never surprise them. And you
keep calm."

We pass a field where five or six big horses are
running. All sweaty, they gallop near the fence,
their manes and tails blowing in the wind.

"I don't see any mountain lions now, but look
at them run," I say.

"They're just playing, getting their exercise," Aunt Maggie explains. "The boy horses, the geldings, are saying, 'Hey, I'm bigger than you. I'm faster than you!' Just like kids on a playground. They challenge a new horse, too, to figure out who's boss. They chase him till everybody's tired. Then they all start grazing together like good buddies. Horses like to know who's in charge, but they also like the herd to stay friendly."

We turn in where the sign says Kentucky Farms. Right by the gate, two horses are standing close. One horse has its teeth in the other horse's neck. I don't like the looks of it.

"They're biting each other!" I say.

25

Aunt Maggie laughs. "It's just a nibble. A horse can't reach her own neck to scratch when it itches, so a friend does it with her teeth. When I brush a horse's neck, she knows I'm a friend, too. Maybe she even thinks I'm a horse!"

The car stops by the stable and we get out.

"Come on, Kyle," Aunt Maggie says. "I want you to meet Barney. He's 28 years old, but he's my baby. The day he was born, I was in the stall — touching him everywhere, messing with him, talking to him, the way a mother horse would in the wild. It's called imprinting. Now I'm his family. He lets me do anything I want with him."

It's dim inside the stable. There's a strong smell, but it's a good kind of strong. I hear the soft sound of a horse blowing air through its nose. Aunt Maggie greets horses she knows on the way through the barn.

"Hello, Blaze," she says. "Stay back, Kyle, she's looking for a treat. I never give treats in my hand. A horse might accidentally bite, trying to find a sugar lump. I give Barney a pat on the neck as a reward."

I hurry past, hiding the apple in my pocket.

"Hi, Johnny boy," Aunt Maggie says at the next stall. "Look here. Johnny's knocked holes in the wall and chewed on the door. He's throwing his head up and down."

"What's his problem? Bad mood?" I say, stepping past carefully. "I'll stay out of his way."

"That's just the problem. His owners have been away. Nobody works with him. Oh, he goes out to pasture at night with the other horses. He's fine then. But he's bored all day. Horses need a purpose in life, just like we do. They need their friends — horse friends or people friends."

I'm thinking how sad that would be, just stuck in a stall with nothing to do. "Can I pet Johnny, Aunt Maggie?" I ask suddenly.

"Better look at his tail first," she says. "And his ears. The ears always go back before a horse bites. It's a warning. Horses don't bite or hurt each other much in the wild — they read the tails and ears, and stay away. It helps keep peace in the herd."

Johnny's tail is swishing. His ears are laid back. "Next time, Johnny," I say.

27

And now we're at Barney's stall. Aunt Maggie calls his name, and the pony comes and puts his brown head on her shoulder.

I wish I could give Barney the apple.

"Ready to saddle up, Kyle?" Aunt Maggie looks to see if I'm still scared.

"Sure, Aunt Maggie, what's first?" She hands me a brush and shows me where to start.

"Brushing's first, every time. And what's last is that apple you've been trying to hide in your pocket. We'll give it to Barney in a bucket when the lesson's over. No harm in that."

I'm smiling now. It's great to be in horse country.

# Glossary

*Bond*

**Archaeologist:** a person who studies early people and their way of life.

**Bond:** a close relationship or friendship.

**Breed:** to give birth to offspring.

**Browser:** an animal that feeds on leaves, young plants, and other vegetation; grazer.

**Chariot:** an ancient horse-drawn, two-wheeled vehicle used in war or races.

**Companionship:** friendship and company.

**Communicate:** to talk to each other.

**Cultures:** groups of people with similar lifestyles, traditions, and beliefs.

**Digest:** to change food into a simpler material that can be absorbed by the body.

**Domesticate:** to train an animal to live in a shelter built by humans.

**Extinction:** the end of the life of a kind of animal.

**Groom:** to clean or brush an animal.

**Harness:** to control.

**Ice Age:** a period of time thousands of years ago when glaciers or ice covered a large part of earth's surface.

*Groom*

**Permanent:** lasting; unchanging.

**Prehistoric:** the period of time before written history.

**Steppe:** a large grass-covered area, often called a plain.

**Tack up:** to put a harness on a horse.

**Vulnerable:** unprotected; exposed.

**Wildlife:** animals that live in the wild away from humans.

*Chariot*

*Extinction*

# The World of
# PETS

*Arctic Circle*

**North America**

*United States*

*Atlantic Ocean*

**South America**

*Pacific Ocean*

**Antarctica**

Poland

Europe

Mongolia

Asia

Africa

Indian

Ocean

Australia

# Animals are Amazing!

## Sea Star

Sea Star grips the rocky ocean bottom near shore. Waves crash over her, but she holds on tight. Tiny suckers underneath her five arms keep her in place. The suckers are on the tips of hundreds of little tubes that Sea Star uses as feet to crawl along the ocean floor.

The ocean waves carry the smell of clams to her. Sea Star is always ready for a meal. Her muscles pull water inside her body. Her tube feet fill like little balloons, and their suckers grab onto the sea floor. Then Sea Star squeezes the water out of some of her tube feet to pull herself forward. By pumping water in and out, Sea Star creeps closer and closer to the smell of clams.

When Sea Star reaches her goal, she climbs on top of a clam. The clam snaps its two shells closed, hiding its soft body. Clamping on with her tube feet, Sea Star tries to pry the shells open. She pulls and pulls, but the clam's strong muscles hold tight. Finally, Sea Star budges the shells apart.

Sea Star flips her stomach out through the mouth on her underside and into the tiny gap between the shells. She squirts chemicals that soften the clam's body. When the clam turns soupy, she swallows her meal. All that remains are two empty shells. After finishing her meal, Sea Star clings

All around the world, animals roam on the earth, in the sky, and under the water. Come explore the fascinating world of animals through a unique collection of stories inspired from the pages of *CLICK*® magazine. Travel with us as we meet many types of animals and discover all the amazing ways they enhance our world.

**$17⁹⁵ each**

**Titles in the Animal Series**

**BUGS**

**PETS**

**WATER ANIMALS**

**WILD ANIMALS**

Carus Publishing Company